T009913:

SKINNYdip

SKINNYdip poetry

edited by

Susan Paris & Kate De Goldi

illustrations by Amy van Luijk

ANNUALink

TERM 1

TERM 2

TERM 3

TERM 4

TERM 1

Free verse

school sucks but at least ur friends are there

u can only walk around the suburbs so often on bright days so hot
the concrete crackles n text ur friends at malls and fields and malls again

before u start to get bored of running
out of things to do &

miss the lush red first kiss of a fresh 1B5
and the girls in ur class with lip gloss scented stationery

& the boys who draw on their mates legs with sharpies &
also i guess learning new things every day

school sucks but all my friends are there
spreading colds as quick as climate change

no one shares germs with me in the holidays

in the holidays my outside voice wears jeans with grassy knees
& watches compilation youtube videos on the highest volume

& i walk around the suburbs on days so hot the ice block
drips down my wrist   with sticky fingers it feeds the crackling concrete

Vanessa Mei Crofskey

Begin with a mountain (山).

I remember shimmering peaks beyond the harbour back home,
Tararua, sugar-dusted on winter-blue mornings.

I remember a mountain hiding behind clouds above the town
where Mum grew up, Kinabalu, sacred mountain.

Begin with a body of water (水).

Dad took me walking every Sunday down by the Waikanae estuary,
where sand cliffs crumbled into the current.

Dad came here when he was little, too, where the river meets the sea,
where Te Ātiawa ki Whakarongotai are guardians of the land and water.

Where are you from?

I'm always avoiding the question.
I can give you the long answer or the short.

I was born in the city where rare yellow pōhutukawa drop
their lemon threads along the shore, where her aloes

spread themselves over the gravel, where congee simmers
on the stove and rain falls sideways on the hills.

Where are you really from?

Tauiwi means *visitor, foreigner, one who comes from far away.*
Hakka 客家人 means *guest people.*

Pākehā, tauiwi, Hakka, Chinese.
I hold all of them in me.

Where are your ancestors from?

Aunt Maureen drew a family tree. It begins in London in 1839
with Charles Plummer Powles and in Tasmania, 1845,

with Eliza Cay Adams. He proposed to her
inside a cream-coloured house at no. 22 The Terrace
while she was doing the dusting.

Remember how you came to be here.

I tried to draw a family tree but I couldn't untangle the roots.
When my grandmother, a young girl, stepped onto the boat

that would carry her across the South China Sea,
some records and memories were lost to the deep.

Acknowledge the people who were here long before you.

Taranaki Whānui ki Te Upoko o Te Ika, who travelled south
in waves of migration from their ancestral home of Taranaki

to Te Whanganui-a-Tara — who were then forced out
of Te Aro and Pipitea by the English.

Acknowledge this land that has welcomed you home.

Put 山水 together and you can see the harbour:
its cold waves, small islands.

They don't belong to me but I belong to them.
Some of us carry oceans wherever we go.

Nina Mingya Powles

Lunchtime Offence

In assembly, we are told bullrush
is banned.
So we crouch by the trees
hunt black beetles in the grass
yell and sprint
with fistfuls
to shove down shirts.
Lucy grabs Bao by the collar
Max tackles Thomas
I jump
on top.
Is that bullrush
you're playing? Mrs Moffat
stands over
our body tangle, her mouth
in a line.
Nah, we say,
brushing green-stained
knees.
Beetle crush.

Amy McDaid

Free verse

Alphabet poem

Straying Focused

AM — Another Monday. On the
board: *Brainstorm BODMAS and give examples.*
Could BODMAS be to do with
diet? Isn't body mass a thing?
Every Good Boy Deserves
Fruit. All Cows Eat
Grass. Those are mnemonics. AHARS (Acronyms
Help Aaron Remember Stuff) is an acronym.
I just invented it. And
JIT-it. I often Just-In-Time it.
KISS stands for Keep It Simple Stupid, but,
LOL, lots of mnemonics don't. Does
My Very Extravagant Mother Just Sent Us
Ninety Parakeets help you list
our solar system's planets? Pluto's not even a
planet now. Could it be an acronym? I mean
Qantas stands for something.
Radar, laser, sonar, and
scuba are acronyms too. Saying
the letters is an initialism, e.g., TV, TGIF, and
USA. Remember Richard Of York Gained Battle In
Vain or Roy G. Biv? There's a rainbow outside now.
Where does it end? What's the question again? WYSIWYG.

James Brown

kutu

like grains of sand
at the shoreline
of the scalp

they lay seven eggs a night
firmly glued
to strands of hair

off the head they
take up to three days to die

essa may ranapiri

Street Fighter

Just past the gate
the footpath's a cloud
squeezed out like the tea towels Mum hangs
up in the morning, eh? All grey

and dark
and splotchy too.

We pretend to listen to the teacher's
last reminders over the bell

but we

'bout to walk home with mates now,
might as well be adults —

and we

'bout to walk near some sun now,
it's wagged the whole day —

and our

phone's on HP, Mum said we can't fix
the screen yet,

can always hide it from the rain, though.

The bell's already gone
two minutes of a day too crunch-soggy and woah
yep
still so muggy
we're rushing forward

Free verse

like ants on Nutella sandwiches
crusts cut off and shaped
into benches all along the tech block.

Once we throw the ringing behind us
it's hop
        skip
and jump the cracks
with zig-zag weeds
and Roman sandals
and ew
toes

and ew
crooked lines

nah, ew
keep the count
and don't step
on odds or else you're out.

Cars dribble past us
like baby vom —
nothing
   then
      blues as
we get spat on
by headlights

keep driving, creeps,
keep driving

they're honking
big as a hadouken
and quick as one, too,
quicker than the fingers
we pull behind them.
Keep driving, creeps,
we whisper 'til they've turned,
then we shout.

The cement's about to rain,
not at the dairy though

a dark blue shelter
covers the five-second
walk to the spacies
just outside the shop door.

That's old-school, bro.
That's no charger styles, eh?

Standing tall like a Queen's guard
surrounded by a few kids in our year
and two oldies in high school uniform
vs-ing each other
red and blue
Ken and Ryu

they go downdownleft
and up right left
and down left third-button mash
watching the fight from the shoulders
and the down diagonal forward punch
so everyone oohs and ahhhs
in the light at the end of their fists

my go next

    they laugh us back
the ring of school uniforms
tightens like a scrunchie

but, why not

they say our hands
are so dainty
that they'll swat us away
and we're mad but quiet with it
since our cousin's up soon
and he'll own the winner, easy.

We squeeze past inside
pick out the ten-cent lollies we'll scoff
before getting back

counting coins out onto the counter
a tinny knock by the two-dollar bags
of snakes and marshies

we only have $3.50

but
that'll fill a bag with rabbits
when our new magic trick
is learning
to want and want to change
the metal to mallow

for the rest of the walk home.

Like seagulls, some of the kids
flap closer to us
lollies clutched in our fists
they ask for some
we laugh and sing

nah, bro!

past all the picket fences

nah, bro!

come play spacies then! they shout

nah, bro!

Laughing
out of breath
at the end of the street already
swapping lollies between us
just a left right down 'til home

power walking
to make sure we're on time
to pull the washing off the line
before Mum wakes up for the night shift

shoving lollies
all the way home.

Amber Esau

School caretaker

I get up at dawn. One of those early wakers.
At the school by six, I work unseen,
which is how I like it. What I make is

soon unmade. I guess my mistake is
I take care. The grounds so neat, tidy, and green.
But here they come, the troublemakers.

They trample all over my fine green acres.
The enamel in the toilets gleams. It's clean.
But not for long. Not with these jokers.

I come from a long line of caretakers.
The kids are all right. They're OK. I mean,
when I forget where the spade or the rake is,

they'll find it for me. On my birthday, a cake is
presented by the food-tech class in the school canteen.
It's sometimes a flop, but I thank the bakers.

And the cake has green icing, and for my sake a
tiny lawnmower and a tiny seated figurine
a bit like me, with its tiny cap, its red windbreaker.
They know I care. I'm the school caretaker.

Tim Upperton

Villanelle

Class 3B, 1974 (front row, third on left)

I see her just as she looks away.
       She's crossing her arms, like a good girl on the mat,
her classmates sit and stand nice and straight with shiny hair,
       and the photographer says, *Got it*, and they're caught.
Then everyone groans, *I think I shut my eyes!*
       Did you smile? With teeth? and they laugh, noisily,

like parents. She blinks away the flash.
       As she walks back to class, bag on one shoulder,
she fiddles with a loose button on her dark blue school cardigan.
       (That morning, was she running late,
arriving as the bell rang — slow dong dong dongs —
       sliding into her seat behind her flip-top wooden desk

and wanting to hide in the girls' after lunch
       to escape the photo?) She doesn't want a photo,
not while it's her time of the month, her skin is bad,
       her uniform stinks under the arms.
I want to catch her eye and say *I get it, I know*,
       but she's looking at something behind the photographer —

Free verse

her least-favourite teacher walking past the door,
        a thought she had, the clock on the wall —
and then it happens, flash, and she's caught.
        (I wonder if she smiles in her class photo next year,
how long her favourite book stays her favourite,
        what part of her face gets wrinkles first …)

Hey, I want to say, *come on, while we still can* —
        let's spend all our coins on lolly mixtures, use up
all our felt-tips, show each other our favourite cartoons,
        roll down hills over onion weed, climb some trees,
hang upside down from the monkey bars,
        laugh and cry over silly little things.

                                        Jane Arthur

Please excuse my strange behaviour

sometimes …
… my hair
grows fast as bamboo / my muscles
flicker like astonished fireflies / my mouth goes sweet
the air sweet the water sweet / my eyes get teary like
all the sons
have returned at once from overseas to their
beautiful ailing mothers and   the wind the wind /
my feet are wings and my wings are wings too
real wings of feather and hollow bone / my jokes
are all necessary yet my silence is iconic
my silence is greedy & my silence is the last biscuit   that
nobody will take my silence
is a pet snake
harmless
really
my silence
rattles in my body …
sometimes …
uh
um
hello
do you want some of my chips?

Sam Duckor-Jones

Free verse

TERM 2

People Give Me Advice about Dealing with My Frenemy

'Be the bigger person,' they said. So I became a mountain.
Along came my frenemy in tramping boots —
his legs were tired, he couldn't get phone reception.
I considered flattening myself out into a nice easy plain.
Instead I got steeper. Became some pretty challenging terrain.

'Keep your cool,' they said. So I turned into a prodigious icicle
and, when I got bored of that, a little tray of ice cubes.
When my frenemy asked what I was doing, I just
made a funny cracking noise.

'Don't stoop to his level,' they said. So I took the bus
to his level. When I finally arrived, I told my frenemy
in detail about my trip — how, in my darker moments,
I lost all faith in public transport. 'The council needs to fix this,' I shouted.
I went on for ages and ages and ages and eventually
my frenemy sighed and got his dad to drive me home.

Free verse

'Talk to him,' people urged. 'Talk to your frenemy.'
So I recounted the entire plot of a movie he hadn't seen.
I told him that if all of Earth's history were compressed
into a single day, he would have been alive
for about 0.0001 seconds.
I told him all about the life story of a cuttlefish
at which point my frenemy began to roll his eyes and laugh.

People give me advice about dealing with my frenemy.
But our frenemy-ship doesn't follow ordinary logic.
We have annoyed each other onto a whole different planet of logic.
Sometimes we just sit there, together on our planet,
talking about nothing much. Throwing bits of stars
at each other, drawing silly faces in the atmosphere,
and being annoying together.

Ashleigh Young

After the First Instruction

Ka karanga te kaea
'Taringa whakarongo!'
                    and so
          as one
we listen.

'Taringa whakarongo!'
is always the first instruction.
When the kaea calls to listen,
          that is what we do.

                    We listen in an old hall
                    called the whare wānanga
                    because it knows so many things
                    and we are there to learn
                    and to practise.

          There is a polished wooden floor
          we call Papa for the earth.
          The ceiling we call Rangi
          for the sky.

                    Between the earth and sky we learn
                    there is a dance of life forever unfolding
                              everywhere around us.

And as we learn
we see
that haka celebrates this dance
          and demonstrates
          the boundless energy
               of its existence

Free verse

where every action
every movement
has meaning
and purpose
and therefore

must be made with certainty
and authority
to show
that we know
what we're doing.

When the kaea calls 'Ki mua!'
we move forward.
When the kaea calls 'E tū!'
we stand firm.
When the kaea calls 'Kia rite!'

we   prepare.

When the kaea calls 'Kia mau!'
we take a firm hold
of the moment
and we make
the moment ours.

When the kaea calls 'Tūwaewae takahia',
we do not step clumsily or carelessly
or heavily for attention
but instead will carry ourselves
sure footed
nimble
fleet and light

perhaps as pīwaiwaka

skip and flit

from side

to side

and here

and

there

and

any
where

they

care

to

be

remembering

as

they

go

along

the ancient story of the war
between the land birds
and the sea birds

and who it was that first advanced
with his unflinching wero eager to confront
the shrieking gulls and skewer menace
as just another cheeky chance to have

a bit
of
fantail fun.

But if the kaea calls
'Waewae takahia … kia kino nei hoki!'
we will step heavily!
We will stamp our feet with full ferocity!
Be as fierce as we can be.
Raise the dust!
Shake the earth!
Dent the ground with our presence.

And if as we stamp
we make bold ruru eyes
kia kino nei hoki
as fierce as can be
wide round and all seeing
moon bright and burning

aglow in our own heads
we will then see
all who come to us
from every side and we
will even see into their hearts
and know their intention

and by the thunder of our stamping
and our unblinking gaze

they will know ours.

Ben Brown

Lunch Experiment

Monday.
Sandwich filling:
butter, Marmite, pūhā,
raisins, mince, jam, cornflakes, tuna.
Don't eat.

Tuesday.
In my desk it
sits and twitches. A slight
curl appears. A faint odour. Flies
hover.

Wednesday.
A definite
curl sets in. Flies settle
in the middle. Is that a trail
of ants?

Thursday.
The curl bends to
a U. The smell is now
a test. The flies lay eggs. The ants
make nests.

Friday.
Flies and ants now
trapped in the curl's pungent
O. It's ready to eat as a
spring roll!

James Brown

Rondel

History Lesson

A good or a bad thing happened here.
We should spread the news around.
There are probably bones beneath the ground,
but no one seems to care.

The past can only stand and stare.
If only it could make a sound!
A good or a bad thing happened here.
We should spread the news around.

Year after year after year after year,
and the bones are starting to make a mound.
We stand on the top and gaze around.
Breathe in, breathe out. The view is part of our atmosphere.
A good or a bad thing happened here.

Bill Manhire

Oral History Project:
Aunty Madds remembers when they got rid of five-cent coins

Okay, on Thursdays after school Zoe has her guitar lesson
and we have hip hop, but not till four, so no rush —
Zoe waits while we use the school loos to change.
Then we walk so slow we kinda fall over sideways
once or twice, and we get to the dairies at twenty past
three. There are two, across the road from each other

but we can only go to one 'cos Zoe stole gum from the other —
she got caught, and they banned her to teach her a lesson.
We try and fail to look innocent as we go past —
you look guilty as if you whisper or giggle or rush
so we look guilty as, all of us squinting sideways,
wondering if the owners will ever change.

I've never stolen anything. Except spare change
from round the house, abandoned on some surface or other.
I just stand nearby and you don't even see it glide sideways
into my pocket — I can't give you the magic lesson —
I never reveal my tricks — go teach yourself — you can't rush
these things — how to acquire two dollars just by walking past.

I have to remind you that all this is happening in the past,
when everything is different, especially the change.
A twenty-cent piece is huge, a fifty cent huger, and everyone's in a rush
to use up their five-cent coins before we have to start using other
weirder, littler coins, and no five cents at all — let that be a lesson:
the seemingly solid facts of your life are wedged in sideways

Sestina

and might dislodge the moment you turn your head sideways
to check Zoe's watch and see that it's gone half past —
time to start making decisions, then get to our class and her lesson.
We take our sweet time, but our choices rarely change
at the pick'n'mix — we're particular — won't settle for anything other
than perfect when it comes to curating our sugar rush.

It's important to try to avoid the after-school rush —
can't concentrate if we're all getting jostled sideways.
We need peace to pick out our bottles and bears — other
kids are chaos — that's why we let so much time slip past
before we go in and ask the owner to count up our change.
This isn't school and no one wants another maths lesson.

Then we gotta say bye to each other — a crash always follows a rush.
You'll keep learning that lesson till you're old like me, casting a sideways
glance at your past and seeing that's one truth you'll never change.

Freya Daly Sadgrove

Free verse

Why I need to skip school today

My schoolbag's missing. I can't find my left foot.
I think I have a headache? I think I broke my leg?
There is a leaf on the road and if I step outside
I will definitely slip on it and break all of my legs.

My books are missing. I looked outside and saw a cloud in the sky
and I think that I might get rained on. I looked outside and saw
an unidentified flying object in the sky and I think
that I might get alien-invaded on.

The school bus is missing. The flying object looked like a cloud,
but they can't be sure that it was a cloud, and to be on the safe side,
I heard they cancelled school today. I can't decide what to wear.
I can't decide what music to listen to. I can't decide if I'm a goth or not.

School is missing. School actually decided to take the day off,
and I'm thinking of doing the same thing. Buses are cancelled.
Roads are cancelled. Yesterday my teacher said that I've learned
everything there is to learn and I don't need to bother coming back.

I'm missing. It's true, I looked down to put my shoes on and I just
wasn't
there.
I can't find myself, I've looked in all the usual places (top bunk, kitchen,
under the house) but it's no use, I'm definitely missing and in these circumstances
there's no way, absolutely no way
I can go to school.

Oscar Upperton

Waiting in the School Office

The blue stapler sits
beside Mrs Cook's right hand,
its fangs made ready.

With her other hand
she swats at a wayward fly.
The telephone rings.

Underneath your chair
a thumbed piece of bubblegum,
still sticky with spit.

Lynley Edmeades

Haiku series

Great-grandad Rants about 'Current Affairs'

News! Where is it if not in newspaper, black type a printer set?
      The internet.
If there's a custard emergency or yoghurt issue,
some armed blasted insurgency in Mogadishu,
or a celebrity opened their beak and deigned to speak to pondslime,
where is it?   Online.
And sport? To what wireless does one sear one's ears to hear the footfall
of jelly-legged idiots prancing after a football?
Or if some goon lobs a Frisbee, or a cherub swats a golf tee, SLAP?
Where do you find that crap?
      That app.
In my day was the news ever fake?
      No! Every dawn the front page said SHEEP TRAPPED IN LAKE
      or GIRL DRESSED AS MERMAID or THE WEATHER'S A BIT HOT
      or TOWN ERECTS STATUE OF GIGANTIC APRICOT.
But now if there's no news, then what?
      Before they flip the channel on
      get a panel on.
What if no one's listening?   The news must be shrieked!
What if journalism's dead?   The news must be leaked!
They have every minute of the year to fill,
and with what?   Codswallop, hogwash, humbug, and swill.
What is news anyway?   Young ladies and lads, comrades,
      Look up from your doodads and iPads.
What is it, news?   Whatever sells ads.

Nick Ascroft

Free verse

TERM 3

Eulogy for the class frog

This is a sad day.
Is that what I'm meant to say?
Guess she was okay ...
now she's gone away. Hurray?
Sorry, can't hide my delight,

I know you're all quite
sad but can I be forthright?
Her tongue gave me frights,
flicking, flying in the night.
It's not a big secret why

today I won't cry ...
why this is no sad goodbye ...
The class frog and I
never did see eye to eye
because I am the class fly.

Oscar Upperton

Acrostic

Exercise 1.3: Write an Acrostic

Shoes left untended / unshined / lifting apart from the sole
Come summertime they'll be in the bin / until then
High school calls for rigorous homogeny / a wash of navy and magenta
Outfits uncomfortable / learning to say something about ourselves /
      maybe for the first time
On our way to sit on the field at break / pick and twist daisies into chains
Lounging in button-up-polycotton-collared shirts / in unappealing colours

Unlikely combinations of jewellery / smaller is better / easy to hide
Never quite dry / heavy woollen sweaters over top / throw them
In the dryer / QUICKLY / before you go / even though Mum says not to
For real / what's the point of a uniform as an equaliser / if you can still tell everyone
      is different
Out the front door in the morning / everybody readjusts / just trying to look
      like themselves
Roll up a skirt band or trouser leg / add make-up / which will have to be
      scrubbed off later
Might get in trouble for coloured hair / even though it washes out eventually

Kōtuku Titihuia Nuttall

Meatballs and Mandarins

It isn't the sun they are attended by today
but damp socks and soggy windows.
Even the lunch bell is muted in the dank air
as it blubbers its way across the quadrangle.
The teacher pushes in her chair, picks up
her umbrella and is staffroom-bound.
The long lunch hour stretches out
like a clammy pie bag left on the wet footpath.

They form clusters: the boys reach
for a ball and take turns throwing it
with half-formed sentences across the room.
Catch! Ollie yells as the red orb slaps the window
and water starts to drip, pooling on the sill
where below, a group of girls gather
beside the heater, sharing slices of mandarin
and corners of a fleecy sage blanket
recently released from inside a schoolbag
where it was clandestinely stuffed that morning
after a conversation about rain over porridge.

Free verse

The girls take turns playing truth or dare.
I dare you to ask Ollie for a bite of his Subway …
An exclamation of *Ew*! echoes through them
as Ollie shoves the rest of his meatball sub
into his gob, a shred of lettuce lolling on his lips
as he screws up the wrapper and throws it
and the ball across the room.
The boys take turns ignoring the girls
while the girls pretend they don't notice.
It's as if the whole world has been pushed
inside these walls and for the hour, no adults exist.

The bell goes and the teacher boomerangs
back to her desk, banana-caked and caffeinated.
Pick up that wrapper please, Ollie, and put the ball away.
The boys start to lower the volume and themselves
towards the desks and the girls take turns pushing
the last corner of the blanket back into the bag,
the scent of mandarin peel and a stray sliver
of lettuce trapped inside its folds.

Lynley Edmeades

My First Big Hit

~~let it go~~
~~let it go~~
~~let it go~~
~~I'm here in slo-mo~~
~~baby doncha~~ know
~~let it go let it go let it go~~

~~take my heart~~ take my heart ~~take my heart~~
~~you're tearing me apart~~
~~I don't know what to do or where to start~~
~~oh baby my heart~~

~~you cut me like a knife~~
~~you're not even my wife~~
shut up mum
~~I'm down on my knees~~
~~begging you please~~
please shut up mum

rpt

Bill Manhire

Strike-out poem

te ngahere kūwao/the untamed forest

The library is the root of the problem. It is where the world bends
soft around corners and swings
yelling 'make haste', 'make haste' on the only horses
I've ever ridden,
      saplings that expanded
exponentially, exploded
like the big bang over and over again except
they are mini big bangs and you're not allowed those
in language;
      you are in a cavern
of wall-to-wall words. A fortress
some feel imprisoned, stuck
inside knowledge made by
others feel unlocked, broken
      open and illuminated
like in te wehenga, when Rangi and Papa split
wrenching up story between them —
a thousand trunks of gnarled
branches able to replicate and imitate
leaves multiplied and generations born;

Free verse

pūrākau times, when decisions
sprung from the tōtara
and the maire and all the noble trees;

voyaging times, when the North crisscrossed
the South and they renamed the creeping
vines where their tales met;

steam and steel times, when the teeth
of each hoof chewed patterns into land
marking the gallery of time

by the stars that come out during the day
to compete with the sun for brightness
and a multitude of leaves
with a million tiny riders
	gallop the pages that caught them.

Anahera Gildea

PE

This morning we're going to climb a rope.
The rope's hooked to the ceiling of the gym.
To make things a little more challenging,
we've coated the rope with melted butter.
To encourage you to try your hardest,
there's a pool full of hungry piranhas
beneath the rope. Did you know piranhas
can jump? We didn't either! Not until
9.45 a.m. Of course we've phoned
Philip's parents. The hospital says he'll
be fine! You will too. Maybe don't look down.
Did we mention that there's boiling lava
beyond the pool? It's difficult to get
boiling lava these days. Isn't Bunnings
great? What did we just tell you? Don't look down!
The higher you climb, the further you go
from the boiling lava and those hungry
piranhas. Focus on success! Your name
on the school's honours board! Failure is not
an option. Please, don't look down! That way lies
lava, piranhas, and bits of Philip.

Tim Upperton

Blank verse

Sole to Sole

Fahhhhh, man.
I'm
hungry.

        I'm straight up
        hangry.

Got any food?

        Sole, if I had any food
        it'd already be in my mouth.

Sad guy.
—

—

Gotta dollar?

        Nah, g.

I gotta dollar.

        Congratulations.

Egg.
If *you* gotta dollar
we could use *my* dollar
go get us a two-dollar scoop of chips at that place by the beach.

        Sole. I told you — I got *no* dollar.

Reckon if we ask
they'd give us half a scoop
for a dollar?

Dialogue poem

Like
if we ask really nicely.
Like
'Please, Sir.
We only gotta dollar.'

> Pffffft.
> Sole.
> As *if.*
> You've seen their scoops.
> They're stingy as.

Yeah,
true.
Guts.

> Yeah.

—

—

Fahhhhh, man.
Look at that afakasi kid though.
He's eating that Boston bun
like a lion
eating a deer
they just killed
on one of those nature shows.

> Fahhhhh, man, he's *always* got food.

You see his nana at lunchtime?

Nah?

Bro.
She brought him
K
F
C.

To school?

Yeah, man.
Walked straight up to him
in the middle of the quad.
Gave him a three-piece quarter-pack, man.
Upsized.

How do you know that?

Cause I asked him for some chips.

Oooooh, shame.
Did he give you any?

Like
one.

One chip?

Yeah, bro.
One
chip.

Fahhhhh.
Sad guy.

Yeah, sad guy all right.

—

—

Hey!
Sssssssssht.
Sole.
—

—

Sole?
Sssssssssht?
Don't pretend you can't hear me
just cause you're wearing
AirPods.
I know you can hear me.

                                 What?

Gizza bite?

                                 Of what?

Your bun.

                                 But it's almost finished.

Yeah, we can see that.
That's why we wanna bite.
Before it's finished.

                                 —

                                 —

Come on, man.
Me and my uso here,
we're starving.

                                 So am I.

Bro.
You had KFC already.

                                        I gave you some chips at lunchtime.

Seriously?
You gave me
one.
One
sad
stinky
chip.
But that was ages ago.
That's like
ancient history.
Like a mummy in a pyramid in ancient Egypt ancient history.
—
                                        —

—

Go on, bro.
Please.
Gizza bite?

                                        —

                                        —

                                        Fahhhhh.
                                        Fine.
                                        Here.
                                        Finish it.
You sure, bro?

                                        You want it or what?
Oh, shot, bro.
You the man.
Yeah. You the man.

                                        Victor Rodger

Pot Plant

Something small and hot went boom
Through silky stars, out spun Earth
Cells formed membranes, blue-green bloom
Forests towered, fluff gave birth

Through milky stars, out spun Earth
Remember when the asteroid hit?
Then forests flowered, apes gave birth
Over wastelands, new life knit

Remember when the asteroid hit?
Then wolves changed rivers, whales weaved
Over deep sands, new life knit
Later, came these plastic leaves

Dams changed rivers, highways weaved
Cells formed membranes, fungi bloomed
Later, came these plastic leaves
Something small and hot went boom

Rata Gordon

Pantoum

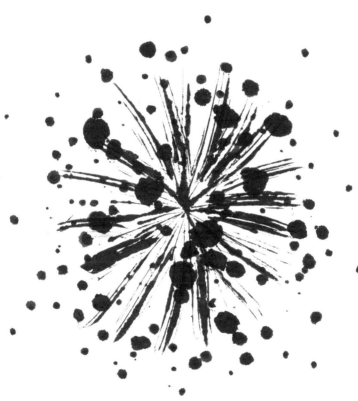

Full-spectrum Career Highlights

I am a painter
I've painted everything
I painted everything blue
My blue phase

I've painted everything
Blue fridge, blue banana
My blue phase
Then there was my yellow phase

Blue fridge, blue banana
Yellow fridge, yellow banana
This was my yellow phase
& the yellow phase grew into the blue & I began a green phase

Yellow fridge, yellow banana
Green fridge, green banana
The yellow had grown into the blue & began a green phase
Whole rainforests in an afternoon

Green fridge, green banana …
It wasn't working
I tore down whole rainforests in an afternoon
& entered my most famous phase: red …

Nothing was working

Pantoum

My painting was irritable & unwanted as a pimple & audiences said: no
I had entered my most famous phase: red
But I persevered & rebranded it as a phase for apples & fire engines

It was an irritable phase unwanted as a pimple but audiences said: yes
Yes to red fridge, red banana
a phase for apples & fire engines
& the red grew & grew till it touched the yellow & began my orange phase

Red fridge, red banana
Orange fridge, orange banana
The red grew & grew till it touched the yellow & began an orange phase
& it touched the blue phase to begin purple

Orange fridge
Purple banana
I touched the blue
I am a painter

Sam Duckor-Jones

In the school garden

When you start with seedlings, say only five leaves,
they're large as life and wickedly green.
A grandma lifts one up, between thumb and finger
from the seed tray, while us kids make the grooves
for carrot seeds. Carrots make us grow like mad
while the grandmas go to pot (to pot and repot
for the plant sale) and while the teachers lift each
growing child one level to the next.

What we're heading for — kids and plants —
are gardens of our own where we can toss
seed around to start something green.
Our bones will know, as we travel to full height,
that the sanest, wildest colour on earth
brings us hope and kick and life.

Dinah Hawken

Sonnet

the bed in the sick bay

i'm littler than most
made to fit
this small room
with lime-green walls.

i've seen everything
in my five years here.

blood noses can be messy
sports days, carnage
tummy aches and wheeze
my usual day.

i know the seven types of poo
on the Bristol Stool Scale
off by heart.

worst is when they spew on me
but when i hold their bodies
feel them tremble
it's hard to stay mad.

Free verse

some i never see again
but many become friends
we lie back
stare out the window together
listen to the thud
of kererū bodies landing
in strong breeze

exhale.

but nights   i am alone
an empty mattress
waiting for the next touch
the next need
the next breath.

Renee Liang

TERM 4

The Hypochondriac Packs

so I'm packing for camp and I'm cacking my pants
and I reckon my brain is like, crawling with ants
and my dad says to chill and that all will be well
but a week in the bush is my personal hell

I have hay fever, asthma, and nut allergies
and like, probably some other awful disease
which I bet I'll succumb to out there in the wild
and my school will be guilty of killing a child

but they want us to bond with the natural world
it's like, give me a break, I'm an indoorsy girl
is it too much to ask for a door and four walls
and a functioning phone with my doctor on call?

so I'm making a spreadsheet for all of my stuff
I'd say four or five suitcases should be enough
but my heart's beating fast and my armpits are damp
'cos there's only two months to get ready for camp

Freya Daly Sadgrove

Free verse

YouTube Academy

Some nights, I wait for the sun to go down
trampoline, on my back, both of us star-bound
while the darkness rises, I put you down beside me
your soft voice guides my pointer finger to Orion, Southern Cross, Matariki.

At the table, we have the most fun painting together
you show me how to mix and blend colours
and layer them with water and oils and observations,
we mull, practise, trace — watch how Monet or Picasso did it
then do studies of landscapes and lilies and our parents.

Our supplies spread across the floor in afternoon light,
we macramé plant hangers, knit beanies, make earrings
with glass beads so fine my fingers ache
although I prick myself with the needle a few times
and drop a stitch every once in a while
I am grateful to know a little bit of what you know.

On warmer days, I take you to the gardens,
where tropical plants scramble up over themselves
towards sun-kissed glass, with hothouse vigour,
and flowers through my earbuds
you take each apart
turn their unpronounceable names
into small, clear notes.

Sitting on my bed, willing the world away from my door
watching video essays (you make your way through every esoteric subject I adore)
ethics and culture and philosophy, Galileo and gravity,
then we do meditation and yoga, end the day perfectly before —

you become a pile of white noise

a great soothing swell

the kind I fall asleep to.

Kōtuku Titihuia Nuttall

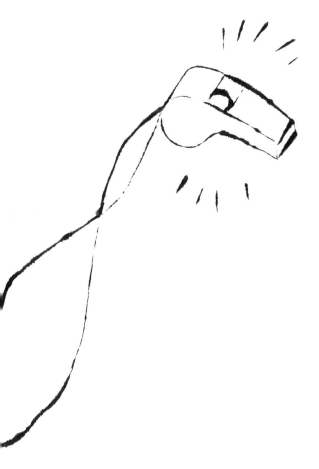

Free verse

There's always someone

There's always someone
who runs the wrong way
right off the field
& straight into a geography lesson

There's always a teacher
who blows a big whistle
& talks about rules
& then just goes
      & breaks them

There's always someone
who goes on & on about the game plan
before the game
but never remembers
when they really really need to

There's always someone who says
there's no I in team
       & then gets really angry
when you say
    there's no
   U
  there
either

& then there's
me, saying to anyone
who'll listen that you can turn team into

tame, into meat, into me right there — *look*!
way out at the end of

the line

Bill Manhire

Cinquain

Dad Helps with Maths Homework

He does.
But helps himself.
Engrossed, he shushes me.
He says come on, don't be a dope!
He is.

Nick Ascroft

At the pool with Epeli

It is the day the pool opens. Everyone
is excited, but especially my friend Epeli.
'Just play it cool,' I tell him.
'I am playing it cool,' he says
while trying to fit last year's swimming cap on his head
and accidentally ripping it in half.

'Please try not to make a big scene,' I tell him
before diving neatly into the water.
When I surface, I see Epeli
doing the dive he calls 'Mr Colbert'
where he spins slowly through the air
with his hands sternly on his hips. Mr Colbert
glares at us from the grandstand.

I grab a pool noodle. 'Let's have a swordfight,' I say,
but Epeli only wants to do backstroke.
'You may not know this, but I am actually
a backstroking champion,' he says
and starts windmilling all over the pool on his back,
generating a lot of froth but very little momentum.

'Get out of the road, Epeli,' people shout
when he backstrokes into them. Epeli only stops to say,
'Did you know that backstroke was first swum
in the 1900 Olympic Games in Paris and the race was won
by a German man named Ernst Hoppenberg?'
I try to tell Epeli that backstroke is the worst stroke

and that he should be doing butterfly, a far superior stroke
that was invented in the 1930s,
but Epeli backstrokes away from me at a funky angle
and ploughs right through someone's game of Marco Polo
and through someone else's complicated underwater dance routine.
I see Mr Colbert shouting and waving his arms.

When Epeli comes back, he announces that he is going to be
the first boy to backstroke the Cook Strait.
He looks at me very intently, his goggle eyes
all round and shiny. 'Will you follow me
in a boat and be my support person?' he asks.
I think for a moment. 'Okay,' I say.

Ashleigh Young

I'm sorry for the bad handwriting the bus is bumpy

I want to write it all down before I forget the best part was slicing through the water in the kayak on my own M. didn't go kayaking she was worried about leaking she had her period she told me like it was a big secret I don't know why if I got my period I would tell the whole school OK maybe not but I wouldn't be weird about it I'm most looking forward to spooning my dog not having a shower not sleeping in my bed and not getting up at 6.30 a.m. the showers were lukewarm they had concrete floors and spongy rubber and bits of old grass to stand on Mr D. told us how a maggot hatched out of his hairline I still don't know if he was serious even though he said it was true I grew a new muscle in my arm because it hurts from rock climbing it was fun even though I wasn't in the same group as C. I felt like Spiderman eating tinned peaches was good Mum never buys them I grew some new freckles over there is the person I want to kiss I'm not saying who but they are sitting next to the person I'm pretty sure they want to kiss which sucks my hair tastes like sunscreen Mrs G. had hairy legs by Thursday and P. said she should shave them and she said he should shave his eyebrows she said to police body hair is rude and obnoxious and antisocial I wish she hadn't explained it and that he turned up on Monday without eyebrows patting the soft bit of fur between the eyebrows on my dog's face is actually what I'm looking forward to most when I get home

Rata Gordon

JavaScript's School Report

There are those who say *terrible* things about JavaScript.
Many of these things are true. JavaScript's simplistic approach
is standard behaviour. It would accept almost anything
but interpret it in a way that was completely different
from what I meant. Mistakes are facts of life,
still, there's no need to wage a war.

Promises have been part of JavaScript for a while.
It allows clearly nonsensical things without complaint,
such as computing true * `"monkey"`.
Often nonsense will merely produce `NaN`
(not a number), while the program happily continues,
convinced that it's doing something meaningful.

Another problem is JavaScript's regular expressions are
rather dumb. I recommend writing a separate function.
This can be useful for putting the hat on the
opposite side of the orbit. It leaves space to
overcome some of JavaScript's shortcomings.
The moral is that the program can be expressed
in both unreadable and readable ways.

JavaScript is still a work in progress.
It is a box with a lock. You can get at it
only when the box is unlocked.
After working with it for a while,
I have learned to actually like JavaScript.

James Brown

Found poem

```javascript
var isNorkInProgress = (x)
=> x === 'Javascript' ?
true : false;


const isWorkInProgreess =
(code) => code ===
'Javascript';

var javascript = { !?:
("@ill"), a: ["work" in


["progress"]]};
```

Kua Tangi te Pere

E ngā atua, e ngā tini āhuatanga o te ao,
kua whāngai mai ki a mātou
i tēnei māra mātauranga, māra tikanga, pā harakeke hoki —
titiro mai nei kia puta ai mātou.

Kua tangi te pere, tukua atu mātou —
kua whakapakari i ō koutou ārahitanga.
Ora roa ake ngā kawekawe o te aka matua
e toro atu ai ki mua, ki muri
kia mau tonu ai tātou.

Kua tangi te pere, tukua atu mātou —
e rere ana ki te taumata, ki te ārai rākau,
kia whatu ai i ngā muka tangata.

Kua tangi te pere, tukua atu mātou —
kua puaki te tūmanako o te reanga hou nei,
ka tae mai te koa ki te whenua.

Tukua atu, tukua atu rā,
kua wātea i ngā huarahi mā tātou,
arā, kia kōkiri ake ngā puananī
ki te tī, ki te tā.

Koinei te wao nui a Tāne.
Ko Ranginui e tū iho nei
Ko Papatūānuku e takoto ake nei.

Tihei mauri ora.

Karakia

The Bell Has Rung

To the guardians, to the elements,
this garden of knowledge, this solid ground,
and this whānau that has raised us —
pay attention, here we are.

The bell has rung, release us —
strengthened by your guidance
we take our place in the continuum
that stretches into the future
and the past.

The bell has rung, release us —
soaring to the peak, to the treetop canopy,
woven together.

The bell has rung, release us —
the hopes of this generation
expressed in the land.

Release us
the path has been cleared —
let the wind-dispersed seeds rush forward
in all directions.

This is the great forest of Tāne.
Ranginui is above
Papatūānuku is below.

This is the breath of life.

Anahera Gildea

A NOTE ON POETIC FORM

Each of the poems in *Skinny Dip* has been written according to the conventions of a particular poetic form. The following is a quick guide to some of the highlights.

Rondels

All poets love the rondel! Not really. This is what Bill Manhire had to say when he sent his one to *Skinny Dip*: 'What a ridiculous, bathetic form!' Elsewhere, the rondel is said to offer an 'exciting structure for new poets to play with'. You decide.

Rondels can be traced to France and the fourteenth century. The form varies, but generally, a rondel is short: two quatrains (a four-line stanza) followed by a quintet (five lines) or a sestet (six lines). That first stanza is important because it contains two lines that act as a blueprint. Take a closer look at Bill's poem on page 43. 'A good or a bad thing happened here/ We should spread the news around.' He repeats these lines at the end of the second stanza. According to the poetry lawmakers, either one or both of these lines then need to appear a final time at the very end. Bill opted for just the one so he could underscore his main point: people interpret the past in different ways. Was an historic event good or bad? It all depends on how you see the world.

Rondels also rhyme. Usually ABBA ABAB ABBAA.

Nothing to do with the band.

Pantoums

Rata Gordon and Sam Duckor-Jones have both written pantoums (pages 72 and 74). And while they play loose with the rules, they stick to the main ones. Each of their last lines is the same as the first, and each stanza is a quatrain. Officially, the second and fourth lines of each stanza ought to reappear as the first and third lines of the next stanza. Rata did this, kind of — but then chose to play around. 'Through silky stars, out spun Earth' becomes 'Through milky stars, out spun Earth.' And 'Then wolves changed rivers, whales weaved' evolves into 'Dams changed rivers, highways weaved.' You could say reading a pantoum's a bit like learning to solve a Rubik's Cube. Subtle shifts reveal fleeting patterns that are quickly replaced.

Sam's subtle shifts sometimes involve tense, but he also tweaks here and there, bending the rules with inexact repetition so that the lines in question can have a conversation. 'My painting was irritable & unwanted as a pimple & audiences said: no' becomes 'It was an irritable phase unwanted as a pimple but audiences said: yes'. Although this repetition becomes more wayward as the poem progresses, the overall structure holds true. Sam respects the pantoum … but he's still the cube master, doing what he needs to do to say what he needs to say.

The pantoum comes from a Malaysian form, the *pantun*. Like the rondel, the form is over six hundred years old. The first pantoums were folk poems, which were much shorter (often only four lines), rhymed, and usually sung. The pantoum eventually made its way to other countries, such as France, Britain, and Aotearoa New Zealand, where writers made the form their own.

Villanelles

The villanelle is another highly structured form for poets who like a challenge: it contains five tercets (three-line stanzas) and a quatrain, with two repeating rhymes and two refrains. Again, there are lots of rules about all this, and again, our poet (Tim Upperton) declines to fully play ball. He says yes to the tercet and quatrain, no to exact repetition — though his poem 'School caretaker' (page 26) does play with sound. Tim uses two rhyme schemes: the 'wakers'/'make is'/'mistake is' pattern (set A); and 'unseen', 'green', 'clean', etc. (set B). Villanelles use an ABA rhyme scheme in each tercet, with the final stanza following an ABAA pattern. It's easy to spot this structure in Tim's poem, and notice the way he sometimes spreads the rhyme over two words ('wakers' rhymes with the later 'mistake is').

With all that repetition, the villanelle's often associated with obsession of one kind or another. One of the most famous villanelles ever written, 'Do not go gentle into that good night', is about defying death, and while not obsessed, exactly, it's clear Dylan Thomas is seized by a powerful longing:

that death can somehow be outrun. To drive home this point, he chooses to repeat the line, 'rage, rage against the dying of the light'. By the final stanza, it's reading like compelling (if futile) advice! Tim Upperton would argue he's not obsessed by school caretakers, either, but he still thinks the form is a good match for his poem. 'A villanelle isn't helpful for telling stories,' he says, 'but it does work well for certain subjects, such as a poem about a person who mows lawns and cleans toilets. Every day, over and over.'

Blank verse

A poem that doesn't rhyme and is written in a regular meter is called blank verse. Meter is the basic rhythm of a poem — the te-*tum* te-*tum* te-*tum* bit. Iambic pentameter has five *tums* (stressed syllables). Be warned: these kinds of poems are often quite serious. Check out Milton's *Paradise Lost*. Tim Upperton's 'PE' (page 64), also written in blank verse, isn't serious at all, and the rhythm jumps about. He says only one line uses perfect iambic pentameter. See if you can find it!

Free verse

If writing a rondel, pantoum, or villanelle is like struggling into a beekeeper's suit, writing free verse is like slouching round in your pyjamas. There's some formality (i.e., not naked), but with so much room to move, the restriction barely registers. That's because free verse has no rules. There's no need to rhyme or write stanzas of a certain length. There are no rules about meter, and the poem's structure can be anything at all. Free verse allows poets to find their groove. The American poet Robert Frost didn't approve of free verse. He said it was like playing tennis without a net.

Free verse contains all the usual features of poetry: careful attention to language, figurative language, rhythm and music, intentional line breaks. It also has many different subsets. There are list poems, erasure poems, prose poems, strike-out poems, dialogue poems, and concrete poems, many of which can be found in this book. People trace free verse back to the King James Bible. A few centuries later, Walt Whitman came along, one of the first poets to throw himself headfirst into the form when he wrote his collection *Leaves of Grass* (1855).

Free verse became especially popular in the early 1900s, a time known as the modernist era, when writers — and artists — big on experimentation took great pleasure smashing their tennis balls right outside the court. Denis Glover, Allen Curnow, Ursula Bethell, and Robin Hyde wrote some of Aotearoa New Zealand's most celebrated poems in free verse.

Alphabet poems and acrostics

It's fair to say the alphabet poem and dreaded classroom acrostic are close cousins, but occasionally, good things do come from a banal start, and 'Straying Focused' (page 17) is a fine example. As a reminder, an alphabet poem and acrostic go like this: each line starts with a letter of the alphabet, or a stem word, as the poet works their way diligently down the list … unless you're James Brown, who pulled out three letters from the end because who can be bothered with x, y, and z? Though of course James is way cleverer than this. He's merely faking failure, a witty flourish so he can point back to the poem's main idea. James understands the challenge of writing in this form. He knows how to use the architectural plan thrust upon him to stealthily make a creation entirely his own.

Sestinas

Did Freya Daly Sadgrove draw the short straw when she ended up writing *Skinny Dip*'s only sestina? (See page 44.) 'Turns out sestinas are hard as,' she says. The form is undeniably complex: six stanzas of six lines each (those sestets again), ending on a three-line envoy (a fancy word for a summary or dedication). That's the simple part.

The fancy footwork kicks in with the six words that end each line. Freya's first stanza contains 'lesson', 'rush', 'change', 'sideways', 'past', and 'other'. The rules demand that she commit to these words. They now have to appear in *every* stanza as end words. You'll see in Freya's second stanza she's done this, but note the order. Yes, another rule. Those key words must appear in a particular order that changes from one stanza to the next. Oh, and that envoy? It also needs to contain the six words, two per line, smack in the middle and right at the end. Do the forensics on Freya's poem. She came through.

So. The obvious question: why why *why* the sestina? We asked Freya, an intermittent poetry rebel. She says aside from the fact she'll never stop bragging about pulling this poem off, she did come to like the form *because* of all the weird rules. 'It was like taking the words on a wild goose chase, then bringing them back home.'

Found poems

The editors of *Skinny Dip* are fond of a found poem. All you need is *someone else's* text and a spirit of adventure. Think of it as chancing upon a completed Rubik's Cube, then messing the whole thing up … only writing a found poem is a lot more satisfying than this. You're not turning order into chaos but creating a thing of wonder in its own right. A found poem needs to have purpose and please the ear — and that's not easy when you arrive late to the party. essa may ranapiri used Ministry of Health guidelines for treating nits to write their found poem (page 18). James Brown (page 94) consulted a book called *Eloquent JavaScript: A Modern Introduction to Programming* (clearly, he didn't agree). Both took the occasional liberty with their material (inserting the odd conjunction or changing tense), which is sometimes necessary when it comes to this form.

Odes

An ode is a lyric poem (something that tends to be musical, meditative, and do a deep-dive on big feelings). It's said the form was invented by the Ancient Greeks so they'd have a public way to revere their athletes. Odes were later written to praise anything that took a poet's fancy. Memory. A vase. Autumn. Solitude. Pablo Neruda wrote about his socks. The English Romantic poets, an intense bunch who lived in the nineteenth century, wrote odes to share their observations about nature but really about their emotional crises. Later still, the American poet Bernadette Mayer wrote an ode to menstruation. She was making a lot of points when she did this, one of them surely being that the form needed to move with the times. Kōtuku Titihuia Nuttall agrees. Her poem is about YouTube (page 84).

There are three kinds of odes: Pindaric, Horatian, and irregular. The first two are named after the Greek poet Pindar and the Roman poet Horace. Google them. Pindar wrote in praise of athletes and other heroes; Horace celebrated good food and wine. Most odes, no matter which kind, tend to have a serious or thoughtful tone; the poet is observing something as a way of working towards what it is they really want to say. Kōtuku goes so far as to address the object of her attention, YouTube, in the second person. It feels like her best friend, her solace from the world, and isn't this the poem's true subject? Ashleigh Young's poem is also an ode (page 90). She writes about that very particular kind of joy in late October when the town pool finally opens, although she also celebrates Epeli. Exuberant, unstoppable, half-crazed by the sense of occasion, he's the perfect swimming companion — and the perfect place for Ashleigh to start.

Sonnets

Skinny Dip contains one sonnet: 'In the School Garden' by Dinah Hawken (page 76). Like all sonnets, it has fourteen lines and reflects upon one main idea, with a change of direction in the second stanza. In keeping with tradition, Dinah opens her poem out in the ninth line, and we have our first glimpse of where she's ultimately heading. She switches from what she sees to what she *feels* about what she sees. The poem's not really about kids planting carrot seeds, but she does linger over these details, hopeful we'll take pleasure in them, too. Now Dinah's writing about the full stretch of life, about the miracle of human growth and development and the things we do along the way to find meaning, gardening included.

James K. Baxter (famous for his commune on the Whanganui River) published *Jerusalem Sonnets* in 1970. He believed inspeaking the truth, in 'not hiding one's heart from others', and clearly found the unrhymed sonnet a useful form for this. There are two other kinds of sonnet: the Petrarchan and Shakespearean. Google them!

Tanka and haiku

Both these forms come from Japan, and both tell us something of the Japanese aesthetic: simplicity, space, definitely no clutter. Makes sense when you live in a small country with a population twenty-five times our own. Tanka is one of the oldest kinds of poetry. In the Japanese imperial court, nobles competed in tanka contests, their own take on slam poetry. Like a sonnet, tanka usually contain a pivotal moment that signals a change from thinking about the thing to thinking about the feeling associated with the thing.

Tanka contain thirty-one syllables across five lines in a 5/7/5/7/7 pattern. Haiku are shorter: three lines and seventeen syllables (5/7/5). Both Lynley Edmeades (page 48) and Oscar Upperton (page 55) have written tanka and haiku series. It's a smart way to enlarge on your subject, bypassing what some might consider to be the limitations of the forms.

Cinquains

Poets agree that cinquains are fun! Take a close look at the rules (a variation on haiku and tanka) and you'll see why. They're doable. Cinquains are five lines long and all about the syllable count. Line one = two syllables, line two = four syllables, etc. Read 'Lunch Experiment' (page 40) or 'Dad Helps with Maths Homework' (page 89) to count up the rest. Again, James Brown has sandwiched five cinquains together so he can write about an entire week.

There's a few other things the cinquain writer is obliged to cover: the first line needs to be a noun, the poem's subject. Subsequent lines are meant to describe or elaborate upon the subject, including associated feelings, if you can locate them. And, strictly speaking, line five ought to be a synonym for that initial noun — or some kind of word to sum it up. But by now, we can all agree that poetry rules, while useful, are there to be nudged and bent and sometimes broken.

THE POETS

Jane Arthur lives in Wellington, where she's the co-owner and manager of a small bookshop. Her first poetry collection, *Craven* (Victoria University Press), won the Jessie Mackay Award for Best First Poetry Book at the 2020 Ockham New Zealand Book Awards.

Nick Ascroft lives in Wellington. His latest poetry collection, *Moral Sloth* (VUP), is designed to be a holiday from piety. He and his ex are doing a fantastic job of co-parenting … or will be until the kid is old enough for Nick to micromanage his homework (see page 89).

Ben Brown (Ngāti Mahuta, Ngāti Koroki, Ngāti Pāoa) was born in Motueka in 1962. He's been writing all his life, across all genres, and published his first children's book in 1991. If pressed, he will have something to say about anything. He says his poem 'After the First Instruction' is about 'getting your heart and mind and actions and spirit working together with the world'. Ben reckons his children are his best work.

James Brown lives in Island Bay, Wellington. His household doesn't own a car, but, for your convenience, his poetry is now available in a *Selected Poems* (VUP). 'My *Skinny Dip* poems all involve following formal rules, which I like because rules push your imagination outside its usual boxes. That said, all writing involves careful listening and rewriting what doesn't sound right.'

Vanessa Mei Crofskey is an artist and writer based in Pōneke. She has a collection of poems published in *AUP New Poets 6* and worked as a writer for *The Pantograph Punch*. She's now the director of an art gallery but dreams about running away to the mountains. 'I hung out with my ten-year-old cousin when I wrote my poem for *Skinny Dip*. He was on school holidays, staying at my grandparents. I watched him starfish all over the couch, then wander around outside. I wanted to connect to the feeling of expansion and aimlessness that school holidays invoke, that slight loneliness of not being around kids your age.'

Freya Daly Sadgrove is a writer and performer from Pōneke. Her first book of poetry, *Head Girl*, was published in 2020 (VUP). 'Usually when I write poems, I work quite hard not to follow any "rules", but perversely, I'm also a teacher's pet and a sucker for rules, so I asked *Skinny Dip* for a difficult form — a bit like requesting extra homework. I got more than I bargained for.'

Sam Duckor-Jones lives in Wellington. He has published two collections of poems: *People from the Pit Stand Up* and *Party Legend* (VUP). 'Crushes are wobbly, swirling things, so it's fitting to write a poem about a crush in free verse. And art is my favourite subject, but no one can make a masterpiece the very first time! Practice makes perfect. So the repeated lines of a pantoum are an excellent fit for a poem about painting and making art.'

Lynley Edmeades lives in Dunedin with her partner and young son. Her most recent book, *Listening In* (Otago University Press), was longlisted for the Ockham New Zealand Book Awards. When she's not writing or teaching or playing in a sandpit, she likes to walk in the hills. She wrote her *Skinny Dip* poems in stolen moments, reimagining her own school days.

Amber Esau likes to poet. She is a Sā-māo-rish writer (Ngāpuhi/Manase) born, bred, and still living in Tāmaki Makaurau.

Anahera Gildea (Ngāti Tukorehe) asks zillions of questions and likes to go in search of the answers. 'When I was ten, I rode trees. One sturdy branch in our backyard was my "horse". The libraries of my childhood nourished my imagination, expanded my view of the world, and helped me to forge my identity. Many of the stories I grew up with were pūrākau, or Māori origin stories. Pū is a foundation or seed, and rākau is a tree. From the canopy of these "trees" come our storied histories. In this poem, I wanted to bring together the two worldviews I grew up with.'

Rata Gordon is a poet, embodiment teacher, and arts therapist. Her first book of poetry, *Second Person* (VUP), was published in 2020. She lives in Raglan and can see Mount Karioi through her kitchen window. She enjoyed the process of being commissioned to write poems for *Skinny Dip*. It pushed her to try things she wouldn't otherwise have tried. She says she would never write a pantoum of her own volition. Too tricky!

Dinah Hawken is a poet and grandmother who lives in Paekākāriki. Her ninth collection of poetry is *Sea-light* (VUP). Some of Dinah's friends grow seedlings in the local school garden. She wanted to include them, along with students, in her sonnet. She often wonders why fourteen lines make such a satisfying poem.

Renee Liang grew up in Tāmaki Makaurau. 'I've done all kinds of writing: poems, plays, short fiction, even an opera. One of my most recent works was a play I wrote for my children, who are half Croatian. It's a retelling of an old Croatian folk tale but set in West Auckland. Actors performed the play with puppets and music and a tent made from bedsheets. I'm a children's doctor, so my poem "the bed in sick bay" drew on that experience — spot the medical details! When I write, I like to act, so I tried to imagine myself in the sick bay after everyone had gone home.'

Amy McDaid lives in Titirangi. Her first novel, *Fake Baby* (Penguin Random House), was published in 2020. 'Lunchtime Offence' is the first poem she's written for young readers, a commission that sparked a few memories of her own primary-school wranglings with illegal bullrush.

Bill Manhire is better known as a poet, but he's also published short stories and essays. He founded the famous creative writing programme at Victoria University. He likes commissions. 'They push me sideways from myself. I stop spouting the same old, predictable things. It's a bit like finding yourself in a prison and having to tunnel your way out. You have to work away steadily, but it can be strangely exhilarating.'

Kōtuku Titihuia Nuttall (Te Āti Awa, Ngāti Tūwharetoa, Ngāti Rangatahi, Tsawout First Nation) is a writer and artist from the Kāpiti Coast. She holds an MA in Creative Writing from Te Pūtahi Tuhi Auaha o Te Ao (International Institute of Modern Letters), where she won the 2020 Adam Foundation Prize. She lives by the beach with her wife and cat. 'When I wrote my ode to YouTube, I wanted to show how much YouTube meant to me. It got me through high school and university. As for uniforms, they can be as constraining as acrostics. But sometimes that constraint can help you make something new and interesting and creative that wiggles itself free of any binds!'

Nina Mingya Powles lives in London. Her most recent publication is *Magnolia* (Seraph Press, 2020). 'I was never taught at school how to recite my pepeha — and I was always unsure where to begin since my family comes from many places. To me, my family tree looks more like a river that flows into several oceans.'

essa may ranapiri (Ngāti Wehi Wehi, Na Guinnich) lives on Ngāti Wairere whenua in Kirikiriroa. Their debut book of poetry, *ransack* (VUP), was published in 2019. When writing 'kutu', they had fun playing with words not wholly their own to explore something quiet in that all too common experience of dealing with kutu.

Victor Rodger is a Wellington-based writer of Samoan and Scottish descent. His zombies-in-a-supermarket short film script, *Night Fill*, was recently published in *Landfall*. When he was a poor drama student in the 1990s, he could often be heard asking 'Gotta dollar?' because 1. You could buy pies for a dollar back then, and 2. He was always hungry. In his poem, a boy's grandmother brings him KFC to school for lunch — exactly what Victor's grandmother used to do.

Oscar Upperton lives in Wellington. His first poetry collection, *New Transgender Blockbusters* (VUP), can be ordered online if you can't find it at your local bookshop. 'I was asked to write a funny poem about the death of the class frog.

I really like frogs, so I couldn't find anything funny to say about frog death —
until I realised the one creature who *would* celebrate such an event. Then the
poem came easily.'

Tim Upperton lives and writes in Palmerston North. He's written three
collections of poems. He says that villanelles are easy to spot because of their
weirdness, and while blank verse is less obvious, noticing the stresses in each
line can help. But, he asks, why do blank-verse poets favour five regular beats
per line? Why not six? 'Because that's hexameter, that's why. One theory is
that an iambic pentameter line is about as much as you talk before you need
to take a breath. But everyone's lungs are different. Give it a go.'

Ashleigh Young lives in Wellington. Aside from writing and reading,
she loves running, riding her bike, and swimming. 'I've always marvelled
at ultra-endurance athletes and wished I could be one, but I'm far too lazy
to do the work. A while ago, I watched a great documentary about people
training to swim the English Channel and all the family and friends who
helped them do it. I realised that my character, Epeli, also wants to try
something big like that — he wants to swim the Cook Strait. Unlike me,
though, I think Epeli is actually going to pull it off.'

ANNUALink

Annual Ink is an imprint of Massey University Press
First published in 2021 by Massey University Press
Private Bag 102904, North Shore Mail Centre
Auckland 0745, New Zealand
www.masseypress.ac.nz

Text copyright © individual authors 2021
Design by Marcus Thomas
Cover and illustrations by Amy van Luijk

All rights reserved. Except as provided by the Copyright
Act 1994, no part of this book may be reproduced, stored in
or introduced into a retrieval system or transmitted in any
form or by any means (electronic, mechanical, photocopying,
recording or otherwise) without the prior written permission
of both the copyright owner(s) and the publisher.

A catalogue record for this book is available from the
National Library of New Zealand

Printed and bound in China by Everbest Investment Ltd

ISBN: 978-0-9951407-6-9